Vegetarian Recipes

Easy and delicious recipes for beginners

Table of contents

3

Pumpkin Pot Pie

Ingredients

for Vegetable Filling

1 small sugar pumpkin, roasted
3 large carrots
2 celery stalks
2 cups vegetable stock
1 small white onion (or half of a large one)
1 bunch of kale (about 8 cups chopped, stems removed)
1 can of white kidney beans
4 garlic cloves, crushed
salt and pepper
pinch of pepper
olive oil for sautéing

For the Roux

1 generous pat of butter
2 tablespoons flour
vegetable stock, about 2 ladles full (taken from above)
salt, pepper

for Crust

1 3/4 cup flour
1 stick of butter
2 egg yolks
1/2 cup of parmesan cheese, grated
1/2 teaspoon salt
1/2 teaspoon white pepper
1 egg for egg wash (optional)

Directions

Wash, peel, chop and roast a small sugar pumpkin on 350 F for 10 minutes. Sauté the mirepoix on medium heat with a little olive oil, salt and pepper. Wash and chop the kale, removing the stems. Add to the mirepoix and let wilt on low with vegetable broth. Make a roux: melt butter in a hot pot, add two tablespoons of flour, one at a time. Let that get toasty and fragrant before you add the stock – one ladle full at a time. Mix roux in with remaining filling ingredients. Combine ingredients for the crust with your hands or stand mixer. Roll out dough on a well floured surface in the shape of your oven-proof bowls. Place filling in bowls, don't fill to the brim – you don't want the good stuff to run over! Place crust on top of bowls and pinch edges around the rim. For a shiny looking crust, brush an egg wash over the pie before baking. Bake for 35 minutes on 375 F.

Notes
If the crust don't seem to want to come together – add 2 to 3 tablespoons of cold water.

Roasted Butternut Squash Risotto

Prep time: 15 mins Cook time: 65 mins Total time: 1 hour 20 mins
Serves: 4 servings

Ingredients

Butternut squash risotto
3 tablespoons olive oil, divided
1 small yellow onion, chopped
2 cloves garlic, pressed or minced
4 cups (32 ounces) vegetable broth, divided
1½ cups brown arborio/short-grain brown rice
1 small butternut squash (about 2 pounds), peeled and sliced into ½" cubes
1 cup freshly grated Parmesan cheese* (about 2½ ounces)
½ cup dry white wine, optional
3 tablespoons unsalted butter, diced
1 teaspoon salt, more to taste
Freshly ground black pepper, to taste
Pinch red pepper flakes, to taste

Fried sage
1 tablespoon extra-virgin olive oil
16 to 20 fresh sage leaves, chopped (to yield about ¼ cup chopped fresh sage)

Directions

To prepare: Place your oven racks in the lower third and upper third positions, then preheat oven to 375 degrees Fahrenheit. Line a large, rimmed baking sheet with parchment paper for the butternut squash. Reserve 1 cup broth from your container and set it aside for when the risotto is out of the oven.

Heat 1 tablespoon olive oil in a medium to large Dutch oven over medium heat until shimmering. Add onion and a pinch of salt. Cook, stirring occasionally, until softened and turning translucent, about 5 minutes. Add the minced garlic and cook until the garlic is fragrant, 1 to 2 minutes.

Add 3 cups broth and 1 cup water, cover, and bring to a boil over medium-high heat. Remove from heat and stir in the rice. Cover the pot and bake on the lower rack until rice is tender and cooked through, about 65 to 70 minutes. It will seem pretty dry when you take off the lid, but don't worry!

Immediately afterward, toss the cubed butternut with 2 tablespoons olive oil on your lined baking sheet. Sprinkle with salt and some freshly ground black pepper and arrange the butternut in a single layer on the pan. Roast on the upper rack until the butternut is fork tender and the edges are deeply caramelized, tossing halfway. This took 55 to 60 minutes for me, but start checking for doneness around 40 minutes.

In the meantime, fry the sage: Heat 1 tablespoon olive oil in a medium skillet over medium heat. Once the oil is shimmering, add the sage and toss to coat. Let the sage get darker green and crispy (but not brown) before transferring it to a plate covered with a paper towel. Sprinkle the fried sage lightly with salt and set it aside.

Carefully remove the Dutch oven from the oven. Remove the lid and pour in the remaining cup of broth, the Parmesan, wine and butter. Stir vigorously for 2 to 3 minutes, until the rice is thick and creamy. Stir in the salt, a generous amount of pepper and a pinch of red pepper flakes.

Stir in the roasted butternut. Taste and add more salt and/or pepper, as needed. Divide the risotto into bowls and top each with a sprinkle of fried sage.

Quinoa-Stuffed Acorn Squash Rings

Ingredients

olive oil mister or cooking spray
1/2 c. quinoa, rinsed thoroughly
1 c. vegetable broth
1 tbsp. olive oil
1 medium onion, diced
1 apple, cored and diced
1/2 c. shredded sharp or smoked cheddar cheese
1/4 c. dried cranberries
2 tbsp. chopped sage
2 tbsp. chopped walnuts
salt + pepper to taste
1 egg, whisked
3 small acorn or sweet dumpling squash, cut into 1/2-inch slices (remove seeds & guts)
1 tbsp. butter, melted
1 tbsp. maple syrup

Directions

Preheat oven to 375 degrees. Spray two rimmed baking sheets with cooking spray or oil and place squash rings on sheets.

Cook quinoa in broth according to package directions. Cool slightly.

Heat olive oil in a medium skillet over medium heat. Add onion.

Cook about 10 minutes, or until onion is just beginning to brown. Add apple and cook about 5 minutes more, until apple is softened. Allow to cool slightly.

Combine quinoa, apple and onion mixture, cheese, cranberries, sage, and walnuts in a large bowl. Add salt and pepper to taste. Stir in egg.

In a small bowl, combine butter and maple syrup. Brush tops and insides of squash rings with butter mixture; season with salt and pepper.

Stuff quinoa filling into the center of each squash ring, pressing down to fit as much stuffing as possible without overflowing. Spray tops of squash with oil or cooking spray. Bake 30-40 minutes, or until tops are golden brown and squash is tender.

Whipped Sweet Potatoes

Ingredients

4 large sweet potatoes (about 4 pounds)
3 tbsp. maple syrup
2 tsp. vanilla extract
1/2 tsp. ground cinnamon
salt to taste

chopped candied pecans (optional)

Directions

Preheat oven to 400 degrees.

Pierce sweet potatoes several times with a fork. Place on a rimmed baking sheet and bake until tender and starting to caramelize. The time depends on the size and shape of potato you're using, but it's usually between an hour and an hour and a half. Allow to cool slightly.

Once potatoes have cooled, remove skin. Place potatoes in bowl and whip with a hand mixer at medium speed. Add maple syrup, vanilla extract, and cinnamon and mix until combined. Stir in salt to taste. Transfer to serving bowl and top with pecans, if desired.

French Bread Stuffing with Swiss Chard & Caramelized Red Onions

Ingredients

2 tbsp. olive oil
2 large red onions, halved and thinly sliced
1 bunch Swiss chard (about 1 pound), stems removed and leaves torn into bite-sized pieces
1 (8 ounce) stale baguette, cut into 3/4 inch cubes
1 large egg, beaten
2 oz. shredded fontina or Italian blend cheese
salt + pepper to taste
1 1/2 c. vegetable broth
oil mister or cooking spray

Directions

Heat oil in a large skillet over low heat.   Add onions and a pinch of salt. Cook until caramelized, stirring occasionally at first and more frequently as onions begin to brown. Depending on your stove, this could take between a half an hour to a little over an hour.

Preheat oven to 375 degrees.

Bring a large pot of water to a boil. Add chard and cook 5 minutes. Remove and rinse with cold water. Drain thoroughly and set aside.

Place bread cubes in large bowl. Add egg; toss to coat. Stir in onions, chard, cheese, salt and pepper, and broth. Transfer to 3 quart baking dish that's been coated in cooking spray. Bake covered for 30 minutes. Remove cover, spray top with oil or cooking spray, and bake 15-20 minutes more until stuffing is golden brown.

Rosemary Roasted Carrots

Ingredients

2 bunches of small carrots (about 24), peeled
1 tbsp. olive oil
1 tbsp. minced rosemary
salt and pepper

Directions

Preheat oven to 400 degrees. Toss carrots with olive oil on a rimmed baking sheet. Sprinkle with rosemary, salt & pepper. Bake 20-25 minutes or until tender.

Veggie Burger

Ingredients

2 (15 oz cans) black beans, rinsed & drained
1/2 red bell pepper
1/2 white onion, cut into wedges
3 cloves garlic, peeled
1 egg
1 tbsp. chili powder
1 tsp. cumin
1/2 tsp. salt
1 cup leftover stuffing (make sure it's vegetarian!)
Burger Toppings:
leftover mashed potatoes
leftover green beans or green bean casserole
vegetarian gravy
hamburger buns
Instructions

Directions

Pulse black beans in a food processor until roughly chopped. Alternately, you can mash in a bowl with a fork.

Add red pepper, onions, and garlic to beans and pulse all together in the food processor until a "paste" is made.

Add black bean mixture to a large bowl along with egg, seasonings, and stuffing. Mix together really well, preferably with your hands, so it all becomes incorporated.

Using 1/3 of a cup, divide mixture into patties and fry them up in a frying pan or non-stick griddle on medium heat until brown on one side, about 5-8 minutes. Flip and brown the other side.

Once browned, you can create your burger. Top a hamburger bun with stuffing patty, mashed potatoes, green beans, and gravy. Either top with bun or eat open-faced.

Portobello Mushrooms Stuffed with Eggplant And Gorgonzola

Ingredients

6 6-inch diameter Portobello mushrooms
1/4 c olive oil
4 Japanese eggplants; chopped
6 tb tomatoes, oil-packed; chopped, drained
2 cloves Garlic; minced
1/4 c Dry Red Wine
6 oz Gorgonzola cheese; Crumbled
2 tb fresh basil; Chopped
1/4 c Grated Parmesan; fresh
Original recipe makes 6 Servings

Directions

Preheat oven to 375F. Arrange mushrooms, rounded side down, on large baking sheet. Heat oil in heavy medium skillet over medium heat. Add eggplant, sun-dried tomatoes and garlic. Saute until eggplant is soft, about 8 minutes. Stir in red wine and simmer until liquid evaporates, about 2 minutes. Remove skillet from heat; stir in

Gorgonzola cheese and 1 tablespoon basil. Season with salt and pepper. Spoon mixture evenly into mushroom caps. Sprinkle with Parmesan cheese. Cover mushrooms with aluminum foil. Bake mushrooms for 15 minutes. Remove foil and continue baking until cheese melts, filling bubbles and mushrooms are tender when pierced with sharp knife, about 10 minutes. Sprinkle mushrooms with remaining 1 tablespoon basil and serve warm. Makes 6 servings.

Baked Acorn Squash With Walnuts And Cranberries

Ingredients

1 Acorn Squash, cut in half

½ cup walnuts, roughly chopped

½ cup cranberries, frozen or fresh

3 Tablespoons brown sugar
2 Tablespoons butter

Directions

Preheat your oven to 375F.

In a small bowl, combine the walnuts, cranberries, and brown sugar. Mix well to combine.

Rinse the acorn squash and cut in half.

Using a spoon, scoop the seeds out of each half and discard.

Using a fork, poke a few holes in the bottom and top of each squash half, and then evenly divide the fruit and nut mixture between two halves of the squash.

Top each half with 1 Tablespoon of butter, and place side by side in a square baking pan.

Cover the pan loosely with aluminum foil and bake for 1 hour 15 minutes- 1 hour 30 minutes. (Done with a fork can be easily inserted).

Serve warm and enjoy!

Sweet Potato Gnocchi with Balsamic-Sage Brown Butter

Ingredients

1 1/2 pounds sweet potatoes (yams) halved lengthwise
1/2 pound Russet potatoes halved lengthwise
1 tablespoon olive oil
2 teaspoons kosher salt plus more to taste
Freshly ground black pepper as needed, plus more for garnish
1/4 cup finely grated Parmigiano Reggiano cheese plus more for garnish
1 large egg lightly beaten
3 tablespoons honey
1 1/2 to 2 1/2 cups all purpose or white whole wheat flour
4 tablespoons unsalted butter
12 to 15 fresh sage leaves
2 medium shallots quartered and thinly sliced
3 tablespoons balsamic vinegar

Directions

For the gnocchi: Heat an oven to 425°F and arrange a rack in the middle. Drizzle potatoes with olive oil, season with a few good pinches of salt and a few cranks of pepper, place on a rimmed baking sheet, cut-side down, and roast until fork tender, about 30 minutes.

Set aside until cool enough to handle. Scoop flesh out of skins then pass flesh through a potato ricer (or mash with back of a fork) and stir in cheese, egg, honey, and the 2 teaspoons of salt. Mix in flour, about 1/2 cup at a time, until soft dough forms. Taste and add additional salt, as needed. You've added enough flour when you touch the back of the dough and it is damp but not sticking to your hand.

Turn dough out onto floured surface and shape into a square. Use a bench scraper to divide the dough into 16 equal pieces. Rolling between palms and floured work surface, form each piece into a rope (about 1/2 inch in diameter), sprinkling with flour as needed if sticky. (However, don't add too much additional flour, as too much will make for heavy gnocchi.) Cut each rope into 1/2 -inch pieces. Stop here or, as desired, using your thumb, roll each piece down over the tines of a fork to indent.

Bring a large pot of heavily salted water to a slow boil over medium-high heat. Working in batches, simmer gnocchi until they float then cook and additional 30 (if fresh) to 60 seconds (if frozen). Using a slotted spoon, transfer gnocchi to a clean rimmed baking sheet. Reserve 2/3 cups of pasta cooking water and drain the rest.

For the sauce: Meanwhile, in a large frying pan, melt the butter over medium heat. Once it foams, add sage and cook until crisp and fragrant. Remove sage to a plate and return frying pan to stove. Add shallot and, watching it carefully and stirring often, allow the milk solids to begin to brown and the butter to become fragrant and nutty. Scrape along the bottom to prevent the solids from sticking and burning.

When the butter is brown, immediately remove from heat, and carefully stir in the vinegar (otherwise it may sting your eyes). Stir in pasta and 1/2 cup of the reserved pasta water, return to heat, and cook until just coated in the sauce. Add a lot of freshly ground black pepper, taste for seasoning and finish with additional pasta water, salt, black pepper, the crisp sage, and freshly shaved Parmigiano-Reggiano.

Tip: Gnocchi can be made 4 hours ahead -- let stand at room temperature then dip in simmering water until heated through.

Mushroom Pot Pie

Ingredients

4 ounces (8 tablespoons) unsalted butter

12 ounces mushrooms (approximately 4 cups), quartered (I used crimini, see notes)

2 cups yellow onion (approximately 1 large), finely chopped

¾ cup celery (approximately 3 ribs), finely chopped

1 cup carrots (approximately 1 carrot), finely chopped

2 cloves garlic, minced

½ cup all-purpose flour

1 tablespoon brandy

2½ cups vegetable or chicken stock, either homemade or low sodium

¼ teaspoon sweet paprika

¼ cup heavy cream

optional: ½ teaspoon good quality white truffle oil

leaves from 3 springs of thyme

¼ cup packed flat leaf parsley, finely chopped

1½ teaspoons kosher salt

½ teaspoon ground black pepper

1 sheet puff pastry

1 egg, lightly beaten

Directions

Heat a large dutch oven or heavy bottom saucepan over low heat, and add 1 tablespoon of the butter. Add the mushrooms along with a pinch of salt and sweat them, stirring periodically, to release some of their natural liquid. After the mushrooms have softened up, approximately 3-4 minutes, turn the heat up to medium and allow them to caramelize for several minutes. Remove the mushrooms from the pan, set aside, and turn the heat down to medium-low.

Melt the remaining butter over medium-low heat and add the onions, celery and carrots. Cook for 5-7 minutes until soft, then add the garlic and cook for an additional minute, stirring periodically. Add the flour and cook for 3-4 minutes. Add the brandy, stock, paprika, and cooked mushrooms.

Bring to a simmer and allow the sauce to thicken, stirring periodically, for 3-5 minutes. Stir in the heavy cream and remove from the heat. Add the truffle oil (if using), thyme, and parsley. Stir in the salt and pepper. Taste; add more if desired.

Preheat the oven to 425 degrees F. Divide the filling into 4 souffle-sized ramekins (approximately 4x2 inches) and place on a baking sheet.

On a lightly floured surface, roll the puff pastry thin and cut 4 rounds approximately ½ - 1 inch larger than the width of the ramekins. Brush egg wash on the rim of each ramekin and ½ inch down the sides. Top with the puff pastry, folding the excess over and gently pressing it against the ramekins (a fork can also be lightly pressed against the puff to help seal it to the dish). Brush the top of the dough with egg wash and use a small knife to poke 3 small holes in the top of each pot pie.

Bake for 20-25 minutes, or until the tops are golden brown. Allow to cool briefly before serving.

Vegetarian Vegetable Stew

Servings: 6

Ingredients

2 tablespoons olive oil
1 medium onion, minced
1 medium carrot, minced
1 medium stalk celery, minced
1 medium red onion, chopped medium
9 medium portobello mushrooms (about 1 and 1/4 pounds), stems discarded, caps halved and then sliced 1/2 inch thick
10 ounces white mushrooms, stems trimmed and mushrooms halved
2 medium garlic cloves, mince
1 teaspoon minced fresh rosemary
1/2 teaspoon dried thyme
1/2 cup white wine
2 and 1/2 cups vegetable stock
1 and 1/2 teaspoons salt
1 cup canned diced tomatoes
1 bay leaf
4 large carrots (about one pound), peeled, halved lengthwise, and cut into 1-inch pieces
4 medium red potatoes (about 1 and 1/2 pounds), peeled, quartered lengthwise, and cut crosswise into 1-inch pieces
1 tablespoon cornstarch
1 tablespoon cold water
1 cup frozen peas, thawed
1/4 cup minced fresh parsley leaves
1 tablespoon balsamic vinegar

Directions

1.   Heat the oil in a large Dutch oven over medium heat.

2. Add the minced onion, carrot, and celery, and sauté, stirring frequently, until the vegetables begin to brown, about 10 minutes.

3.   Add the red onion and sauté until softened, about 5 minutes.

4. Add the portobello and button mushrooms, raise the heat to medium-high, and sauté until the liquid the release has been evaporated, about 10 minutes.

5. Add the garlic, rosemary, and thyme and cook for 30 seconds.

6. Add the wine, scraping up any browned bits stuck to the pot.

7. Cook until the wine is reduced by half, about 2 minutes.

8. Add the stock, salt, tomatoes, bay leaf, carrots, and potatoes, and bring to a boil.

9.   Reduce the heat and simmer, partially covered, until the carrots and potatoes are tender, about 35 minutes.

10. Mix the cornstarch and with water to form a smooth paste.

11.   Stir the paste into the stew and cook until the liquid thickens, 1 to 2 minutes.

12.   Turn off the heat, stir in the peas, cover, and let stand until the peas are hot, 3 to 4 minutes.

13. Stir in the parsley and balsamic vinegar, discard the bay leaf, and adjust the seasonings.   Serve immediately.

Roasted Vegetable Galette

For the dough:

2 1/2 cups all-purpose flour
1 teaspoon salt
1 cup cold unsalted butter, cut into small pieces
1/4 to 1/2 cup ice water

Directions

Pulse flour and salt briefly in a food processor until combined. Add butter and pulse about 10 seconds, until mixture resembles coarse crumbs with some larger pieces remaining. Add 1/4 cup of ice water

and pulse until mixture begins to hold together. If it's too dry, add

up to 1/4 cup more ice water until dough holds (but is not wet or sticky).

Remove dough from food processor and shape into a disc. Wrap in plastic wrap and refrigerate until firm, about 1 hour or overnight.

For the filling:

1.5 cups chopped peeled carrots
1.5 cups chopped peeled parsnips
2 cups chopped peeled butternut squash
3 large shallots, peeled and chopped
1 head garlic
~2 tablespoons extra-virgin olive oil, divided
2 teaspoons chopped fresh rosemary, or 1/2 teaspoon dried
1/2 teaspoon salt, or to taste
Freshly ground pepper, to taste

¼ to ½ cup crumbled goat cheese

Directions

Preheat oven to 400°F. Coat a large baking sheet with cooking spray.

Chop carrots, parsnips, and squash into ½" uniform pieces. Combine vegetables (carrots, parsnips, squash, shallots) with 1.5 tablespoons olive oil, rosemary, salt, and pepper in a large bowl and toss to coat. Spread the vegetables on the baking sheet.

Cut the tips off one end of the head of garlic and drizzle the exposed cloves with a teaspoon of oil. Wrap garlic in foil and place on the baking sheet with the vegetables.

Roast vegetables and garlic until tender (they don't have to be completely soft because they will go in the oven again later), about 20-30 minutes. The garlic may need an additional 10-15 minutes in the oven on its own.

Transfer the vegetables to a large bowl. Unwrap the garlic and let cool slightly. Squeeze out the garlic cloves into a small bowl and mash with 1 teaspoon olive oil. Add the mashed garlic to the vegetables and toss to coat.

Reduce oven temperature to 375°F.

Once dough has chilled, roll it out on a floured surface or pastry mat into a 15" circle, about 1/4" thick. Line a baking sheet with parchment paper and transfer the dough onto the sheet. Arrange the roasted vegetables on top of the dough, leaving a 2-inch border around the edges. Sprinkle goat cheese over the vegetables.

Fold the border of the dough up and over the filling to form a rim, pleating as you go. Bake until crust is golden brown, about 50-60 minutes. Serve warm.

Autumn Tart

Tart Crust
120 g (1 1/4 cup) chickpea flour
90 g (2/3 cup) almond flour
40 g (4 tbsp) potato, tapioca or corn starch
2 tbsp fresh thyme, chopped
1 tsp sea salt and black pepper
6 tbsp coconut oil (a little extra for the tart pan)
6 tbsp ice cold water

Autumn Filling
coconut oil or olive oil for frying
1 small red onion, finely chopped
2 fresh sprigs of rosemary
1 leek, thinly sliced (use the green leaves as well)
500 g fresh baby carrots, divided lengthwise
1 small sweet potato, thinly sliced
1 small romanesco, cut into smaller pieces
6 brown mushrooms, sliced
3 small kale leaves, stems removed and chopped
1/2 lemon, juice

Directions

Preheat the oven at 400°F/200 C°.

Making Almond Crust: Combine all dry ingredients in a bowl. Add coconut oil and ice cold water. Using your hands, work dry ingredients towards the center until dough forms. Gather dough into a ball, wrap in plastic, and chill for 30 min.

Press the dough evenly onto bottom and up sides of a large tartlet pan. Trim dough flush with edge of pans. Prick bottom with a fork to prevent it from bubbling as it bakes. Bake until golden, about 15-20 minutes. Prepare the filling.

Making Autumn Filling: Prepare vegetable. Heat oil in a large skillet over medium heat. Add onion and rosemary, cook until turning light brown, then add leek, carrots, sweet potato and romanesco. Cook until brightly colored and starting to turn golden brown, but still crispy. This should take about 5 minutes. Add mushroom, kale and lemon juice, cook for 2 more minutes and set aside.

Serving Autumn Tart: When the tart is done, remove from oven, let cool a few minutes. Fill the tart with the Autumn Filling and serve!

Vegan Thanksgiving Wraps

Ingredients

SWEET POTATOES

2 large sweet potatoes (~300 g | organic when possible)

1 Tbsp (15 ml) grape seed oil

1 tsp fresh thyme

1/4 tsp ground cinnamon

1/2 tsp sea salt

optional: pinch cayenne pepper

CHICKPEAS

1 15-ounce (425 g) can chickpeas, rinsed, drained and thoroughly dried in a towel

1 Tbsp (15 ml) grape seed oil

1 tsp fresh or dried thyme

Pinch ground cinnamon

1 tsp ground cumin

1/2 tsp smoked paprika

scant 1/2 tsp sea salt

optional: Healthy pinch each ground coriander + cardamom

FOR SERVING optional

4 Garlic Herb Flatbreads (or store-bought flatbreads or pita)

Garlic Dill Hummus Sauce

Toasted sunflower seeds or pumpkin seeds

Dried cranberries, chopped

Fresh arugula or parsley

Directions

Preheat oven to 400 degrees F.

Thoroughly wash and dry sweet potatoes, then slice (skin on) into bite-sized rounds/pieces.
Add to a mixing bowl with grape seed oil, thyme, cinnamon, sea salt and cayenne (optional). Toss to coat, then arrange in a single layer on a baking sheet.

To the same mixing bowl, add rinsed, dried chickpeas, and grape seed oil, thyme, cinnamon, cumin, paprika, sea salt, and coriander + cardamom (optional).

Toss to coat, then arrange on baking sheet with sweet potatoes where space permits. (Depending on size of baking sheet, you may need to use a second to accommodate all potatoes and chickpeas).

Bake for a total of 25 minutes, flipping/stirring once at the 15-minute mark to ensure even cooking. You'll know they're done when the potatoes are fork tender, and the chickpeas are golden brown, dehydrated, and slightly crispy. Remove from oven and set aside.

In the meantime, prepare toppings and dressing (if using).
Once potatoes and chickpeas are finished baking, wrap flatbreads in a damp towel and warm in the still warm oven for 1-2 minutes (or in the microwave for 30 seconds) to soften and make more pliable.

To assemble, top each wrap with a portion of sweet potatoes and chickpeas. Add desired toppings, such as dried cranberries, pumpkin seeds, arugula, and Garlic-Dill Hummus Sauce (recipe link above).

Quinoa Stuffing with Apple, Sweet Potato & Hazelnuts

Ingredients

1 cup (212 g) dry Quinoa, cook according to package directions
2 (265 g) Sweet Potatoes, cut into small wedges
2 large Apples, cut into 1/2" pieces (I like Granny Smith)
1 tablespoon Lemon Juice
1/2 cup (100 ml) pure Maple Syrup, divided portion in 1/2
fine Sea Salt
2 tablespoons melted Coconut Oil
a few pinches ground Cinnamon
a few pinches ground Ginger
1 tablespoon fresh Thyme leaves
1 cup Hazelnuts, chopped
Fresh or Dried Cranberries for garnish

Directions

Rinse quinoa. Combine with 2 cups water and a pinch of salt. Bring to a boil and then reduce to a simmer for about 20 minutes until all of the water is absorbed. Fluff with a fork and remove from the heat.

Preheat oven to 400 F with the rack in the middle. Be sure to coat apples with lemon juice so they don't turn brown. Toss sweet potatoes & apples with 1/4 cup of the Maple Syrup, coconut oil and a few pinches cinnamon, ginger and salt. Roast for about 35-40 minutes until tender and fragrant.

Combine the quinoa with the roasted mixture and the remainder of the maple syrup (1/4 cup) in a large bowl. Fold in thyme and hazelnuts. Season to taste with more salt and spices.

Vegan Shepherd's Pie

Ingredients

FILLING
1 medium onion, diced
2 cloves garlic, minced
1 1/2 cups uncooked brown or green lentils, rinsed and drained
4 cups vegetable stock
2 tsp fresh thyme or 1 tsp dried thyme
1 10-ounce bag frozen mixed veggies: peas, carrots, green beans and corn

MASHED POTATOES
3 pounds yukon gold potatoes, thoroughly washed
3-4 Tbsp vegan butter
Salt and pepper to taste

Directions

Slice any large potatoes in half, place in a large pot and fill with water until they're just covered. Bring to a low boil on medium high heat, then generously salt, cover and cook for 20-30 minutes or until they slide off a knife very easily.

Once cooked, drain, add back to the pot to evaporate any remaining water, then transfer to a mixing bowl. Use a masher, pastry cutter or large fork to mash until smooth. Add add desired amount of vegan butter (2-4 Tbsp), and season with salt and pepper to taste. Loosely cover and set aside.

While potatoes are cooking, preheat oven to 425 degrees F and lightly grease a 2-quart baking dish (or comparable sized dish, such as 9x13 pan. An 8x8 won't fit it all but close!).

In a large saucepan over medium heat, sauté onions and garlic in 1

Tbsp olive oil until lightly browned and caramelized - about 5 minutes.

Add a pinch each salt and pepper. Then add lentils, stock, thyme and stir. Bring to a low boil, then reduce heat to simmer. Continue cooking until lentils are tender (35-40 minutes).

In the last 10 minutes of cooking, add the frozen veggies, stir, and cover to meld the flavors together.

OPTIONAL: To thicken the mixture, add 2-3 Tbsp mashed potatoes and stir. Alternatively, scoop out 1/2 of the mixture and whisk in 2 Tbsp cornstarch or arrowroot powder and whisk. Return to the pan and whisk to thicken.

Taste and adjust seasonings as needed. Then transfer to your prepared oven-safe baking dish and carefully top with mashed potatoes. Smooth down with a spoon or fork and season with another crack of pepper and a little sea salt.

Place on a baking sheet to catch overflow and bake at 425 for 10-15 minutes, or until the mashers are lightly browned on top.

Let cool briefly before serving. The longer it sits, the more it will thicken. Let cool completely before covering, and then store in the fridge for up to a few days. Reheats well in the microwave.

Pumpkin Ravioli

Ingredients

1 cup of canned pumpkin
1/3 cup grated Parmesan cheese
1/2 cup chicken broth
1 1/2 tablespoons unsalted butter
Fresh basil or sage, chopped (around 10 leaves)
24 wonton wrappers
Salt and pepper to taste

Directions

1. Mix pumpkin, Parmesan, around 1/4 teaspoon of salt, and a dash of black pepper in a bowl.
2. Spoon about a 1/2 tablespoon pumpkin mixture into the center of each wonton wrapper (see photos for reference).
3. Moisten edges of dough with water (I used a brush, made it super fast and easy!) and pinch opposite sides together to form a triangle. DOn't forget to seal the edges tightly!
4. Place ravioli into a large saucepan of boiling water and cook around 6-7 minutes, drain carefully. (They're delicate!)
5. Sauce: Pour 1/2 cup of broth and 1 1/2 tablespoons of butter in a large pan and bring to a boil. Add ravioli, tossing to coat.
6. Sprinkle with basil or sage, and maybe some more Parmesan!

Stuffed Mushrooms

Ingredients

1 cup wild rice, cooked according to directions
1 Delicata squash, peeled, cubed and roasted
1/2 red onion, chopped
1 stalk celery, chopped
3 garlic cloves
2 large handfuls chopped kale
1/4 cup crumbled feta cheese
4 portabella mushroom caps, gills scraped clean
1/4 cup chopped pecans
S&P to taste

Directions

In a skillet, saute onion and celery in 1 tsp canola oil for 5 minutes. Add garlic and cook for another minute. Add kale and saute until wilted. Remove from heat and mix with cooked wild rice, delicata squash and feta cheese. Season with salt and pepper to taste.

Preheat the oven to 450 degrees and brush portabella mushroom caps with olive oil. Bake for 5 minutes. Flip caps, fill with equal portions of wild rice mixture and cook for 10-15 minutes. Serve hot.

Brussel Sprout Salad

Dressing

3 Tbsp red wine vinegar
2 Tbsp chopped shallot
1/2 tsp dried thyme
1 1/2 tsp Dijon mustard
1/2 tsp honey
1/2 tsp freshly ground black pepper
1/4 tsp salt
2 garlic cloves, minced
1/4 cup olive oil

Combine all ingredients in a jar and shake vigorously until combined. Serve tossed with salad.

Salad:

16 medium brussel sprouts, stems removed and shaved
1/4 of a red onion, sliced thin
sprinkling of almonds
1/4 cup freshly grated parmesan
small handful of dried cranberries
1/2 avocado, cubed

Toss all salad ingredients together. Pour in just enough dressing to lightly coat the salad. Let sit for 30 minutes before serving.

Quinoa, Mushroom, and Zucchini Veggie Burgers

Ingredients

16 oz. mushrooms, chopped
1 zucchini, grated
1 tablespoon olive oil, plus more for frying.
2 cups cooked quinoa (3/4 cup dry)
plenty of salt and pepper

½ teaspoon crushed red pepper (or more, if you like spicy!)

2 cloves garlic, minced
1 bunch green onions, chopped
2 eggs
1 cup whole wheat bread crumbs

Directions

Cook quinoa according to directions.

Saute mushrooms and zucchini in 1 tablespoon olive oil with a generous pinch of salt over medium-high heat. Stir only once in the beginning, and allow liquid from vegetables to evaporate. Continue cooking until vegetables are tender and most of the liquid has evaporated.

Mix cooked quinoa, vegetables, and remaining ingredients in a medium-sized bowl.
Form 6-8 patties with the mixture and fry over medium-high heat in

2 tablespoons of olive oil in a nonstick skillet. Cook for 2-4 minutes on each side, or until browned.

Move patties to parchment covered baking sheet. Bake at 375 degrees for 20 minutes.

Curry-Stuffed Delicata Squash

Serves 3 to 4

Ingredients

For the squash
1/2 cup black lentils – the little French ones that hold their shape
Coarse salt
1 cup white basmati rice
3 delicata squash, halved lengthwise, scraped clean of seeds
2 teaspoons neutral oil
1 teaspoon maple syrup
1/4 cup olive oil
2 teaspoons super fresh curry powder
1/4 cup shredded coconut, preferably unsweetened (but sweetened will work in a pinch)
1/2 cup yellow raisins, submerged for 10 minutes in a bowl of boiling water to plump, squeezed dry
1/4 cup roasted unsalted sunflower seeds or peanuts
Handful coarsely chopped fresh cilantro leaves for garnish

For the dressing
1/3 cup mayonaise
1 tablespoon lemon juice
2 teaspoons curry powder
1/2 teaspoon coarse salt
2 tablespoons neutral oil
1/2 teaspoon sugar

Directions

Preheat the oven to 400°F.

Bring around 6 cups of water to boil in a small saucepan. Add 1/2 teaspoon salt and the lentils. Lower the heat to a simmer and boil for 20 to 25 minutes, until the lentil are soft but not falling apart. Drain in a fine metal sieve. Set the lentils aside

Rinse the rice in several changes of water, until the water runs clear. Place it in a small covered saucepan with 1 3/4 cups water and 1/2 teaspoon salt. Bring to a boil, then give the rice a stir, put the lid on, and place the pot over the lowest possible heat. Cook for 15 minutes, then turn the heat off and leave the cover on the rice for another 5 to 10 minutes, or until you're ready to use it. (If you have a preferred method of making rice, go for it. You'll need 2 cups of cooked rice.) You'll need 2 cups of the rice; reserve the rest for another use.

Place the squash halves in a lightly oiled baking dish. Combine the oil with the maple syrup, then brush the squash with the mixture. Season with a pinch of salt. Place the squash in the oven and cook them for 30-40 minutes, until they're easily pierced with a fork.

In a large, heavy skillet – a cast iron pan works great – heat the olive oil over medium-high heat. Add the onions and cook, stirring occasionally, until they are wilted and slightly brown, about 10 minutes. Add the curry powder and 1/2 teaspoon salt, until the curry powder is very fragrant, about 3 more minutes. Add the coconut and cook for another minute, then add the lentils, the raisins, sunflower seeds or peanuts, and 2 cups of the rice. Stir gently to combine all the ingredients. Remove the skillet from the heat.

Make the dressing: combine the mayo, lemon juice, curry powder, salt, oil, and sugar, and stir well.

Add about 3/4 of the dressing to the lentil-rice mixture and stir to combine. Taste for balance of flavors, adding more dressing or salt, pepper, or lemon juice as needed. You want the mixture to hold together well.

Fill each squash half to overflowing, using about 2/3 cup of the mixture. Return the squash to the oven and bake for 10-15 minutes, until the top of the filling is slightly browned and crisp.

Sprinkle with the cilantro leaves. Serve 2 halves to those with big appetites; 1 half will be enough for smaller eaters.

Tip: The most important part of this recipe is using fresh curry powder. If your curry powder's old and stale, then your dish will be lacking.

Simple Pumpkin Soup

Ingredients

SOUP
2 sugar pumpkins (~2 1/4 cups (450 g) pumpkin puree)
2 shallots, diced (~1/4 cup or 40 g)
3 cloves garlic, minced (1 1/2 Tbsp or 9 g)
2 cups (480 ml) vegetable broth
1 cup (240 ml) light coconut milk (or sub other non-dairy milk with varied results)
2 Tbsp (30 ml) maple syrup or agave nectar (or honey if not vegan)
1/4 tsp each sea salt, black pepper, cinnamon, nutmeg

GARLIC KALE SESAME TOPPING (optional)
1 cup (67 g) roughly chopped kale
1 large garlic clove, minced
2 Tbsp (18 g) raw sesame seeds
1 Tbsp (15 ml) olive oil
pinch salt

Directions

Preheat oven to 350 degrees F (176 C) and line a baking sheet with parchment paper.

Using a sharp knife, cut off the tops of two sugar pumpkins and then halve them. Use a sharp spoon to scrape out all of the seeds and strings (see notes for a link to roasting seeds).

Brush the flesh with oil and place face down on the baking sheet. Bake for 45-50 minutes or until a fork easily pierces the skin.

Remove from the oven, let cool for 10 minutes, then peel away skin and set pumpkin aside.

To a large saucepan over medium heat add 1 Tbsp olive oil, shallot and garlic. Cook for 2-3 minutes, or until slightly browned and translucent. Turn down heat if cooking too quickly.
Add remaining ingredients, including the pumpkin, and bring to a simmer.

Transfer soup mixture to a blender or use an emulsion blender to puree the soup. If using a blender, place a towel over the top of the lid before mixing to avoid any accidents. Pour mixture back into pot.

Continue cooking over medium-low heat for 5-10 minutes and taste and adjust seasonings as needed. Serve as is or with Kale-Sesame topping.

For the Kale-Sesame topping: In a small skillet over medium heat, dry toast sesame seeds for 2-3 minutes, stirring frequently until slightly golden brown. Be careful as they can burn quickly. Remove from pan and set aside.

To the still hot pan, add olive oil and garlic and sauté until golden brown - about 2 minutes. Add kale and toss, then add a pinch of salt and cover to steam. Cook for another few minutes until kale is wilted and then add sesame seeds back in. Toss to coat and set aside for topping soup.
Recipe serves 3-4. Leftovers keep in the fridge for up to a few days, and in the freezer for up to a month or more.

Oatmeal with mushroom onions chickpeas and greens

Ingredients

1 cup old fashion oats
2 cups water
1 cup or so of cooked chickpeas
small onion
3-4 large white or cremini mushrooms
2 big handfuls of chopped greens (kale,spinach, collards, or broccoli leaf.. whatever greens you got!)
1-2 cloves garlic
balsamic vinegar
olive oil
salt and pepper to taste
handful of cashews or some other nut (optional)

Directions

Start by chopping you mushrooms and onions and tossing them with splash of olive oil into a skillet. Sprinkle with salt and pepper and Begin to cook on medium heat.

Grab a heavy bottom pot and bring the water to a boil. Once boiling, dump in the oats, add a pinch of salt, give a little stir and reduce heat to medium low. Stick a lid on pot and leave it alone for about 10 minutes.

Once the mushrooms and onions are starting to cook down, mince up garlic and add in, along with the chickpeas (drained of liquid) and a few tablespoons of the vinegar. Continue to cook until the veggies are browned, the chick peas are hot, and everything tastes good (give it a taste). Lastly, add in the chopped greens and stir around until wilted.

And the oatmeal should be done. (It's done when it's nice and light and fluffy and that water has absorbed)

Grab a bowl, add a big scoop of the oatmeal, sprinkle with salt and pepper, top with a large amount of the veggie bean mixture and top with another glug of vinegar and some of those cashews all chopped up.

Roasted Cauliflower, Mushroom and Goat Cheese Quiche with Quinoa Crust

Ingredients

FOR THE QUINOA CRUST:
1/2 cup quinoa, rinsed
1 cup water
1 egg
1/4 cup parmigiano reggiano (parmesan), grated (optional)
FOR THE QUICHE:
1/2 medium head cauliflower, cut into florets
8 ounces mushrooms, quartered
1 tablespoon oil

salt and pepper to taste
5 eggs
1/2 cup milk or heavy cream
1/2 teaspoon thyme, chopped
4 ounces goat cheese, crumbled
salt and pepper to taste

Directions

FOR THE QUINOA CRUST:
Bring the quinoa and water to a boil, reduce the heat, simmer, covered, until tender and most of the water has been absorbed, about 15 minutes, remove from heat and let sit covered for 5 minutes.
Mix the quinoa, egg and parmesan, press into the bottom of a pie plate and bake in a preheated 375F/190C oven until lightly golden brown, about 10 minutes, before setting aside.

FOR THE QUICHE:
Toss the cauliflower and mushrooms in the oil, salt and pepper, place on a baking sheet in a single layer and roast in a preheated 400F/200C oven until they start to caramelize, about 20-30 minutes, mixing half way through.
Mix the cauliflower, mushrooms, eggs, milk, thyme, goat cheese, salt and pepper, pour into crust and bake in a preheated 375F/190C oven until golden brown and set in the center, about 30-35 minutes.

P.S Use a pastry crust or a brown rice crust in place of the quinoa crust.
Replace the goat cheese with another cheese like aged white cheddar, blue cheese, etc.

Tip: A toothpick will come out cleanly when pushed into the center of the quiche when it is ready.

It is best to let the quiche come down to room temperature before slicing as the goat cheese will be melted when warm making it more difficult to get nice clean slices.

Pumpkin chili with black beans and garbanzo beans

Ingredients

1 tablespoon olive oil
1 large onion, chopped
4 garlic cloves, minced
1 cup pumpkin puree (from the can or homemade)
1 cup canned tomatoes
1 cup vegetable stock or water
1 can black beans (15 oz, 425 g)
1/2 can garbanzo beans (7.5 oz, 212 g) or white beans
1 tablespoon cumin powder (start with half the amount, and add more, to taste)
2 tablespoons chili powder (start with 1 tablespoon, reduce or add more, depending on your tastes and also on how spicy your chili powder is)
salt and pepper

Directions

In a large pot or skillet, cook chopped onion and minced garlic in olive oil for about 5 minutes on medium heat until soft.

Add pumpkin, canned tomatoes (chop them up into smaller chunks), vegetable stock (or water), black beans and garbanzo beans. Add half the cumin and half the chili powder, stir everything well, and season with salt and pepper. Taste your chili, season some more with salt and pepper if needed. Add the remaining cumin (or more) and remaining chili powder (or more), if desired. Bring to boil, make sure to stir all ingredients well together to combine flavors and spices. Reduce to simmer and cook for 20 minutes on simmer.

Serve in soup bowls, garnished with chopped green onion.

Festive Chickpea Tart

Ingredients

1 tbsp olive oil
1 cup onion, diced
1/2 cup celery, diced
4-5 medium-large garlic cloves, minced
1/4 tsp sea salt
Few pinches freshly ground black pepper
2 cups chickpeas, reserve 1/3 cup
2 tbsp freshly squeezed lemon juice
2 tsp tamari
1/2 tsp ground sage
1/4 tsp sea salt
3/4 cup walnuts, toasted
1/3 cup rolled oats (optional)
1 - 10 oz pckg frozen chopped spinach, thawed and squeezed to remove excess water (about 1 cup after squeezing)
1/4 cup dried cranberries
1/4 cup fresh parsley, chopped
1 tbsp fresh thyme, chopped (or 1 tsp dried thyme added to puree)

1 prepared whole-wheat pastry pie crust, thawed
1/2 tbsp olive oil
1 tsp tamari
2 tbsp walnuts, chopped (for topping, no need to toast beforehand)

Directions

Add oil, onion, celery, garlic, salt and pepper in a skillet over medium-high heat. Cook 9-10 minutes, stirring occasionally, until softened and turning golden. In a food processor, add chickpeas (except reserved 1/3 cup), lemon juice, tamari, sage, salt, and sautéed mixture, and partially puree (not fully like hummus, but leaving some chunkier consistency). Add toasted walnuts and oats, and briefly pulse to lightly break up nuts. Transfer to a bowl, and stir in spinach, cranberries, parsley, thyme, and reserved chickpeas. Transfer mixture to pie shell (or lightly oiled pie plate, see note), smoothing to evenly distribute. Combine oil and tamari, and brush over top. Sprinkle on walnuts. Bake in preheated oven at 400 degrees for 30-35 minutes, until tart is golden on edges and top. Cool 5-10 minutes, then serve with cranberry sauce, a spoon drizzling of oil/balsamic vinegar slurry, or other sauce of choice.   Serves 4-5.

Tip: This tart can be made without the pastry crust, if needed. Do not over bake as tart will tend to dry out without a crust.

Apple Cherry Crisp

Fruit Mixture:
2-3 tbsp pure maple syrup (depending on sweetness of fruits, see note)
2 tsp arrowroot powder
2 cups chopped apples (cored and peel removed)
2 tsp fresh lemon juice
2 cups fresh or frozen cherries, stems and pits removed (or substitute more apples or other fruits, see note)
1/2 tsp pure vanilla extract
1/4 tsp cinnamon
1/4 tsp freshly grated nutmeg
pinch of sea salt

Crisp Topping:
1 cup rolled oats (use certified gluten-free for a gf option)
1/4 cup oat flour (use certified gluten-free for a gf option)
2 tbsp unrefined sugar
1/2 - 3/4 tsp cinnamon
1/8 tsp of sea salt
1 tbsp pure maple syrup
1 - 1 1/2 tbsp neutral-flavored oil

Directions

Preheat oven to 350 degrees. For the fruit mixture, mix maple syrup and arrowroot until smooth. In a large bowl, toss apples with lemon juice, then add maple syrup mixture and remaining fruits mixture. Transfer mixture to a lightly oiled baking dish (8" x 8" or similar size). For the topping, in another bowl, combine oats, sugar, cinnamon, and salt. Mix well, then add maple syrup and oil. Work mixture with your hands, then sprinkle it evenly over the fruit, lightly pressing it down. Bake for 38-43 minutes until bubbling around the edges and lightly browned. Remove and cool a little before serving (lovely served with a non-dairy ice cream). Serves 4-5.

Try different fruit combinations:
- 2 cups chopped apples; 2 cups blueberries
- 2 cups chopped apples; 2 cups frozen mango chunks
- 2 cups chopped pears; 2 cups frozen raspberries
- 2 cups chopped apples; 1 cup chopped pears, 1 cup frozen berries, 2 tbsp cranberries or raisins

Lightened Up Vegetable Lasagna Casserole (Gluten-Free)

Ingredients

3 cups coarsely grated zucchini (about 2 medium zucchinis, grated)
1 1/2 cups coarsely grated carrot (about 1 large peeled carrot, grated)
1 teaspoon salt, optional and to taste
1/2 teaspoon black pepper, optional and to taste
1 large egg, beaten (or egg replacer or flax egg)
1 1/2 cups sour cream (or Tofutti)
3 1/2 cups loosely packed shredded cheese, divided (cheddar, American, mozzarella, Ricotta, soy, goat, Daiya, or a favorite cheese blend)
one 16-ounce jar salsa

Directions

Preheat oven to 400F. Line a 9-by-9-inch pan with aluminum foil, spray with cooking spray; set aside.

In a large mixing bowl combine zucchini, carrot, salt, pepper, and pour the egg over the vegetables; toss to coat.

Pour mixture into prepared pan, lightly packing it and smoothing it down with a spatula. Bake for 25 to 28 minutes, or until vegetables begin to show signs of slight browning on top and have firmed up. Depending on how watery the vegetables were, how much salt was added, and how much water they release will dictate baking time. The vegetable crust doesn't have to be well-done or even very hardened, just not watery and juicy.

Spread sour cream over the top of the crust in a smooth even layer.

Sprinkle about 2 cups cheese uniformly over the sour cream.

Drizzle the salsa (I used a very bean and corn-heavy salsa) uniformly over the cheese.

Top with the remaining cheese, about 1 1/2 cups, sprinkled uniformly. Bake for about 35 to 40 minutes or until cheese has browned and top is bubbly and golden. Depending on the kinds of salsa and cheese used, and how browned you prefer your food, will dictate baking times and could cause them to vary widely; let your eyes be your guide and watch for browning.

Allow lasagna to cool for at least 10 minutes before slicing and serving. Lasagna can be stored in an airtight container in the refrigerator for up to 5 days or frozen for up to 3 months. Leftovers can be served cold or gently reheated.

Tomato And Vegetable White Bean Soup

Ingredients

2 Tbsp olive, grape seed or coconut oil
1 large white or yellow onion, diced
3 cloves garlic, minced
1 cup carrots, sliced
1/2 tsp each sea salt and black pepper + more to taste
1 tsp dried basil, oregano and garlic powder
1/2 pound red potatoes, quartered
2 yellow squash or zucchini, sliced
2 14.5 ounce cans fire roasted tomatoes
1 15 ounce can tomato sauce
5 cups veggie stock (add more salt if needed when using reduced sodium)
1 15 ounce can white beans, rinsed and drained
3 cups kale (or other sturdy green), chopped

Directions

Heat a large pot or dutch oven over medium heat and prep veggies.
Add 2 Tbsp oil, then onion, garlic, carrot and stir. Season with salt, pepper and spices and stir again to coat.
Next add squash, potatoes, fire roasted tomatoes, tomato sauce and veggie stock. Bring soup to a simmer and then reduce heat to low and cover. Continue cooking for 15 minutes, then add beans, another pinch each salt and pepper, and stir. If the soup starts boiling, be sure to lower heat to just a light simmer.

Cook for another at least another 10 minutes to let the flavors meld, and then add kale, stir and cover. Cook for 5 minutes more.

Taste and adjust seasonings as needed. Serve with a hearty bread.

Creamy Spinach Salad with Roast Potatoes, Avocado, and Maple Tempeh

Ingredients

organic baby or regular spinach, washed well – your desired amount
smoky maple tempeh
one avocado
roast potatoes (potatoes, olive oil, pink salt)
For the Dressing: mix 1-2 tablespoons of soy-free vegan mayonnaise with 1-2 tablespoons of apple cider vinegar, and 1/2 tablespoon maple syrup – depending on your taste preferences
Optional: splash of lemon juice, sprinkle of smoked paprika

Directions

Roast potatoes. Scrub two to three large organic potatoes and dice into cubes. Toss with 1 tablespoon olive oil and 1/2 teaspoon pink salt, and roast in a 425F oven for 20 to 25 minutes, or until golden brown)

Either in the same oven, or in a frying pan, prepare tempeh – broil for 8 minutes in the oven, or gently fry in a skillet until lightly golden.

Preparing dressing: whisk together mayonnaise, apple cider vinegar and maple syrup.

Toss spinach with dressing.

Peel and slice avocado, and add to salad.

Arrange tempeh and roast on top of spinach, and finish with the optional splash of lemon juice and smoked paprika. Enjoy!

Cumin Apple Chips

Ingredients

2 tablespoons confectioners' sugar
1 teaspoon ground cumin
1/2 teaspoon ground cinnamon
Pinch salt
1 Granny Smith apple (or other tart, sweet variety; we used Stayman Winesap)

Directions

1. Preheat the oven to 200 degrees F and line a baking sheet with parchment paper.

2. In a small bowl, whisk together sugar, spices, and salt until combined. Using a fork or a sieve, dust the baking sheet with half the mixture.

3. Cut apple into 4 large pieces around the core. Discard core and cut apple quarters into 1/16-inch thick slices, using a mandolin if you have one. Arrange slices on the baking sheet in even layers and dust with remaining sugar mixture.

4. Bake for 1 1/2 hours, until slices have shrunk and become golden. Remove from the oven and allow to cool on the baking sheet. Carefully remove slices from the parchment paper and serve as an appetizer or salad topping. Makes about three dozen chips.

Red Curry Roasted Carrot Soup

Ingredients

1 pound carrots, peeled and cut into 1-inch pieces
2 small red onions, quartered
2 tablespoons olive oil
1/2 teaspoon salt
1 teaspoon sugar
1-inch piece fresh ginger, peeled and roughly chopped
1-2 teaspoons red curry paste
2 cups vegetable stock
15-ounce can full-fat coconut milk
Juice of 1/2 lime
Cilantro, optional
Toasted coconut flakes, optional

Directions

1. Preheat the oven to 425°F and line a baking sheet with parchment paper.

2. In a medium mixing bowl, toss carrots, onions, oil, salt, and sugar. Spread vegetables evenly on the baking sheet and roast 30 to 40 minutes, stirring once halfway through, until browned and tender.

3. Transfer mixture to a food processor or blender and add ginger, 1 teaspoon curry paste, and stock. Blend until incorporated. Add coconut milk and blend until smooth. Taste for seasoning and add salt and additional curry paste if you like. Add lime juice and any additional liquid if you prefer thinner soup.

4. Spoon into bowls and serve garnished with cilantro and toasted coconut.

Pumpkin-Leek Stuffing

Ingredients

One 2-pound pumpkin, peeled, seeded, and cut into 1-inch cubes
Olive oil
Salt
3 leeks, white and light green parts only, halved and thinly sliced
1 1/2 cups vegetable stock, divided
1 large sweet onion, chopped
1 large fennel bulb, chopped
2 teaspoons chopped fresh thyme leaves
1/4 cup dry white wine
Pepper
4 cloves garlic, chopped
2 loaves ciabatta, cut into 1-inch cubes
1 cup unsweetened applesauce
1/4 cup chopped fresh parsley

Directions

1. Preheat the oven to 375 degrees F and line a few rimmed baking sheets with parchment paper. Toss pumpkin with a drizzle of olive oil and a generous amount of salt on sheets and roast for 40 to 45 minutes, redistributing occasionally, until tender and beginning to brown. Remove and set aside in a mixing bowl.

2. In a large Dutch oven or casserole, warm 1/4 cup olive oil over medium heat. Add leeks and sauté for 5 to 10 minutes, until they begin to wilt. Add 1/2 cup stock, turn the flame to low, cover, and

cook for 20 to 25 minutes, stirring occasionally, until leeks are completely soft and beginning to turn to mush. Remove the lid and cook uncovered until most of the liquid has evaporated. Season with salt and add to pumpkin mixture.

3. In the same pot or pan, add a little more olive oil, turn the heat to medium-high, and add onion, fennel, and thyme. Sauté for 10 minutes until tender but not caramelized, then add wine and season with salt and pepper. Continue to sauté for another 5 minutes, until vegetables are very tender and alcohol in the wine has burned off. Add to pumpkin-leek mixture. (Note: Everything up to this point can be made 1 to 2 days ahead of time.)

4. When ready to serve, combine garlic with 1/4 cup olive oil. Heat in the microwave 1 to 2 minutes, until oil is fragrant and infused. Toss ciabatta with oil and a generous amount of salt, and turn out onto several rimmed cookie sheets. Toast in a 350-degree oven for 5 minutes, until bread is crisp but not completely browned.

5. Toss bread with vegetable mixture, applesauce, remaining stock, and parsley. Combine well and add any stock as necessary to make bread moist. Let stand for at least an hour for flavors to absorb. Then return to the oven and cook, covered, for 30 minutes. Uncover and cook for another 15 minutes until the top is crusty and brown.

String Beans with Rosemary Pecans

Ingredients

2 1/2 cups pecans
2 tablespoons olive oil
1 1/2 tablespoons chopped fresh rosemary
1 tablespoon sugar
1 1/2 teaspoons ground cumin
1 teaspoon salt
1 teaspoon freshly ground black pepper
1/4 teaspoon cayenne pepper
3 pounds string beans

Directions

1. Preheat the oven to 300°F.

2. Place pecans in a bowl. In a small, heavy saucepan over medium-low heat, warm olive oil. Add rosemary and stir until aromatic, about 1 minute. Pour seasoned oil over nuts, add sugar, cumin, salt, pepper, and cayenne, and stir to coat evenly.

3. Transfer to a baking pan and bake, stirring occasionally, until nuts are toasted, about 20 minutes. Transfer to a plate and let cool completely. (Note: This can be made up to a week in advance.)

4. When ready to serve, heat a large pot of salted water. Cook green beans until al dente, about 5 minutes. Drain in a colander and run under cool water to stop the cooking. Toss beans in a mixing bowl with a little olive oil, then transfer to a serving platter and top with rosemary nuts.

Roasted Pumpkin Wedges

Ingredients

1 small pumpkin (1 1/2 to 2 pounds), cleaned and scrubbed
2 tablespoons olive oil
1/2 teaspoon sea salt
2 teaspoons brown sugar
3/4 teaspoon ancho chili powder

Directions

1. Preheat the oven to 400 degrees F and line a baking sheet with parchment paper.

2. Cut top and bottom off pumpkin using a large chef's knife. Halve lengthwise and scoop out flesh with a spoon (grapefruit spoons work well here). Discard flesh and reserve seeds for another use.

3. Cut pumpkin into 1/4-inch wedges and toss in a large mixing bowl with olive oil, salt, sugar, and chili powder. Arrange in an even layer on the baking sheet and roast for 30 to 40 minutes, flipping halfway, until wedges are soft and caramelized. Allow to cool slightly before serving.

Basil Turnip Hash

Ingredients

2 tablespoons olive oil
2 medium turnips (about 1 pound), finely diced
2 medium Yukon gold potatoes (about 1 pound), finely diced
1 sweet onion, finely diced
1 teaspoon paprika
1 teaspoon salt
1/4 cup coarsely torn basil leaves

Directions

1. In a large cast-iron skillet, heat olive oil over high heat. Add turnips and potatoes and cook about 30 minutes, stirring occasionally, until tender and dark browned on all sides. Add onion, paprika, and salt, and turn the heat to medium-low. Sauté for about 5 minutes, until translucent and sweet. Stir in half the basil.

2. To serve, spoon hash onto plates and top with remaining basil.

Hearts of Romaine with Beets, Pistachios, and Basil

Ingredients

3 hearts of romaine, bases removed and halved lengthwise
1 pound mixed roasted beets, skins removed, halved and cut into 1/4-inch thick wedges
1/4 cup shelled pistachios
1/4 cup loosely packed basil leaves, coarsely torn
1/2 cup roasted garlic vinaigrette
Salt and Pepper, to taste

Directions

Arrange romaine hearts on a platter. Carefully scatter roasted beets over the center of wedges, followed by pistachios and basil. Right before you're ready to serve, drizzle vinaigrette over the top and season with salt and pepper.

Warm Delicata Squash Salad

Ingredients

4 pounds delicata squash
2 medium red onions, halved and cut into thin half-moons
3 tablespoons olive oil, divided
3/4 teaspoon salt
1 tablespoon balsamic vinegar
1 teaspoon finely chopped fresh oregano
1/4 teaspoon crushed red chili flakes

Directions

1. Preheat the oven to 400°F and line a baking sheet with parchment paper.

2. Remove ends of squash and cut in half length-wise. Scoop out and discard seeds and stringy interior (a grapefruit spoon works well for this). Cut squash into 1/2-inch slices and toss with onions, 2 tablespoons oil, and 1/2 teaspoon salt on the baking sheet. Arrange in an even layer and bake 30 minutes, redistributing once during the cooking process, until browned and tender.

3. In the meantime, combine vinegar, remaining oil, oregano, chili flakes, and remaining salt. (It's okay if oil and vinegar don't emulsify.)

4. Transfer squash to a serving bowl and drizzle with balsamic mixture. Garnish with additional oregano, and serve immediately.

Spiced Semi-Sweet Potato Mash with Caramelized Onions

Ingredients

2 tablespoons olive oil
4 large Vidalia onions, thinly sliced
1/4 teaspoon paprika
1/2 teaspoon cumin
Salt
1/4 teaspoon cayenne pepper (or to taste)
2 pounds sweet potatoes, peeled and cut into 1-inch cubes
2 pounds Yukon potatoes, peeled and cut into 1-inch cubes
1/4 teaspoon chili powder
Vegetable stock, optional

Directions

1. Add oil to a pan over medium heat, and spread onions as evenly as possible across the pan. Every few minutes, scrape the bottom and redistribute onions so each gains the maximum amount of surface area. (The intention is to slowly crisp onions by enticing the remaining liquids to sweat out and for onions to sweeten by condensing in their own juices.)

2. When onions are dark brown, but not burnt (about 40 minutes), add paprika and cumin, and season with salt and cayenne to taste. Set aside.

3. In the meantime, place sweet potatoes and Yukons in a large pot

and cover with water by two inches. Bring to a boil over high heat and simmer until fork-tender. Drain and mash in a large mixing bowl.

4. Season potatoes to taste, adding chili powder and any additional cayenne. If mixture is too thick, thin with some vegetable stock. Transfer to a casserole and spread in an even layer. Top with caramelized onions and serve immediately.

Apple Croustades

Ingredients

¼ cup Armagnac, cognac, or rum

¼ cup raisins

½ cup plus 2 Tbs. vegan margarine, divided

5 large tart apples, peeled and cut into ½-inch dice (5 cups)

½ cup sugar, divided

18 sheets frozen phyllo dough, thawed (one-half 16-oz. pkg.)

Directions

1. Pour Armagnac over raisins in bowl. Set aside to plump 15 minutes.

2. Heat 2 Tbs. margarine in large skillet over medium-high heat. Add apples, and sauté 5 minutes, or until beginning to brown. Add raisins and Armagnac, and cook 2 minutes, or until alcohol has evaporated. Transfer to bowl, and stir in 1/4 cup sugar. Cool.

3. Preheat oven to 350°F. Melt remaining 1/2 cup margarine. Brush 12-cup muffin pan (1/2 cup size) with melted margarine.

4. Unroll phyllo, and keep under damp towel to retain moisture. Place 1 phyllo sheet on work surface. Brush with margarine, and sprinkle with 1/2 tsp. sugar. Top with second phyllo sheet, brush with margarine, and sprinkle with 1/2 tsp. sugar. Repeat until you have 6 layers of phyllo sheets, but do not sprinkle top sheet with sugar. Cut phyllo stacks into 4 squares. Press 1 square into 1 muffin mold, letting edges hang over. Fill phyllo "crust" with 1/3 cup apple mixture. Brush edges with margarine, and fold over apple mixture. Brush top with margarine to "glue" top together. Repeat with remaining squares. Repeat layering and assembly with remaining phyllo sheets, margarine, sugar, and apple mixture.

5. Bake croustades 20 to 25 minutes, or until golden-brown. Cool 10 minutes in muffin pan, then carefully unmold, and cool on wire rack. Serve warm or at room temperature.

Wild Mushroom Croustades

Ingredients

3 tablespoons olive oil, divided

1 cup thinly sliced brown onion

2 medium-sized, finely minced garlic cloves

1 tablespoon finely chopped, fresh thyme, plus a couple extra sprigs for garnish

1-1/2 pounds fresh, mixed wild mushrooms, washed, dried and roughly chopped (I used Shitake, Maitake & Oyster)

1/4 cup dry sherry

Sea salt and freshly ground pepper to taste

1 medium to large French baguette

Directions

Preheat the oven to 375 degrees F.

Coat the bottom of a large sauté pan with 1 tablespoon of the olive oil and place it over medium-high heat. Add the onion and garlic and cook until the onions are caramelized, about 15 minutes.

Add the thyme, the remaining 2 tablespoons of olive oil, and mushrooms.

Turn the heat to low, and add the sherry. Then turn the heat to high and deglaze the pan with the sherry, scraping any bits of onion and mushrooms off the bottom of the pan, and back into the mixture. Cook for another 5 minutes or so.

Season with a bit of salt and pepper. Cover and set aside.

Cut the baguette into thin slices (about 1/4 to 1/2-inch) and place them on a baking sheet. Toast them in the preheated 375 degree F oven until they are beginning to turn golden.

Add 1 to 2 tablespoons of the mushroom mixture on top of each toast.

Serve warm with a bit of fresh thyme on top.

Flaxseed Crackers with Hummus

Ingredients

1 3/4 cups flaxseeds (brown, golden, or mixed)
1 medium carrot, chopped (about 2 cup)
4 one-inch pieces fresh ginger, peeled and minced (about 4 cup)
3 medium cloves fresh garlic, minced
1/2 teaspoon cayenne pepper
1/2 cup nama shoyu (substitute tamari or 3 cup miso paste to make gluten free)
Dash of curry powder
Dash of ground cumin
3 tablespoons cold-pressed olive oil
1 bunch fresh cilantro leaves, chopped (about 1 cup)
4 cups water, plus additional (up to 1 cup) as needed

Directions

1. Put the flaxseeds in a large bowl. Combine all the other ingredients with the 4 cups water in a blender and blend well.

2. Pour the blended mixture over the flaxseeds and stir to combine. Allow the mixture to sit for 10 to 15 minutes until it begins to thicken. Stir in more water every 15 minutes until the mixture is goopy and will spread well on a tray but is not too runny.

3. Transfer 2 cups of the mixture to a ParraFlex sheet on a dehydrator tray and spread it thinly with a spatula (or you can even use a plastering float or trowel) until it is approximately 4 inch thick. Repeat on additional trays with the remaining mixture.

4. Put the trays in the dehydrator and dehydrate the crackers for 3 to 4 hours, until the tops are dried.

5. Remove the trays from the dehydrator. To flip the crackers to dry the other side, place an empty dehydrator tray (without a ParraFlex sheet) over the top of one of the cracker trays, hold them both together, and flip them. Then remove the top dehydrator tray and peel the ParraFlex sheet off the crackers. Repeat with the other trays. Put the crackers back into the dehydrator and dry until crispy, 6 to 8 hours.

Sprouted Chickpea Hummus

SERVES
Makes 6 cups

Ingredients

6 cups sprouted chickpeas
For the Tahini Sauce:
2 medium lemons, peeled and quartered
1 cup tahini
1 medium yellow onion, peeled and quartered
3 medium cloves garlic
1/2 cup fresh parsley leaves
1/2 cup fresh cilantro leaves
1 teaspoon ground cumin

1/3 cup cold-pressed olive oil

1 teaspoon sea salt, plus additional (up to 1 teaspoon) to taste

Directions

1. Put the sprouted chickpeas in a food processor and blend well. Remove to a large bowl.

2. To make the Tahini Sauce: Put the lemon first, then the remaining ingredients, in a blender and blend well.

3. Pour the Tahini Sauce into the bowl with the chickpeas and mix well. Taste and adjust the seasonings.

Fig And Olive Tapenade

Ingredients

1 cup kalamata olives- pitted
1 cup dried black mission figs- quartered and stemmed
juice of ½ half of of an organic lemon
zest of one organic lemon
1 cup sauvignon blanc

¼ cup extra virgin olive oil

Directions

Soak quartered figs in wine for at least a half hour and up to 2 hours
Drain figs reserving the liquid
Add figs, olives, lemon juice, ¾ of the lemon zest, and about 1 tablespoon of the wine to the bowl of your food processor and pulse until blended.
Add more wine if the mixture is too hard to blend. Do not over process. It should still have texture.
Finally pulse in olive oil.
Put into a pretty serving dish and garnish with the rest of the lemon zest.
This tapenade tastes great right away, but even better the next day.

Butternut Squash Parsley Dip

Ingredients

2 cups cooked butternut squash
1 cup fresh parsley
2 Tbsp almond, cashew or sunflower seed butter
Zest and juice from 1/2 a lime
1 clove fresh garlic, pressed
1 tsp paprika
1/4 tsp sea salt

Directions

Put all of the ingredients in a food processor and puree until smooth.
If your squash is fully cooked and soft, you shouldn't need any extra liquid but if it's looking thick you can add a bit of vegetable broth or water.

This dip is perfect served warm, when the squash has just been cooked or warmed in an oven. Enjoy it with crackers, toasted pita wedges, cucumber slices or red pepper chunks.

Sun-dried Tomato and Butternut Squash Bisque

Yield: 8 servings

Ingredients

1 medium sized butternut squash
1 teaspoon minced garlic
1 leek, tough green parts removed, cleaned and sliced
1/2 tablespoon olive oil
1 cup sundried tomatoes (not in oil), soaked at least 1 hour and drained
2 cups salted vegetable broth
1 2/3 cup low fat canned coconut milk (or your favorite nondairy milk)
1/2 teaspoon ground cumin
Sea salt and black pepper to taste

Directions

About 1 hour before preparing preheat your oven to 350 °F, slice your butternut squash in half lengthwise and remove the seeds. Sprinkle the flesh of the squash gently with salt and then place face down on a baking sheet. Add about 1/4 cup water to the pan and cook 45- 60 minutes, or until the squash's skin is tender enough to easily be pierced with a fork.

While the squash is roasting, saute the garlic and leek along with the olive oil over medium high heat until tender, about 10 minutes. Set aside.

Once the squash is tender, transfer to a high speed blender (or use a good quality immersion blender or food processor) and puree along with garlic and leek, the sundried tomatoes, vegetable broth, coconut milk, and cumin. Add a little more broth if you prefer a thinner soup. Blend until completely smooth, about 10 minutes. Warm gently if needed over medium heat until desired temperature is reached. Salt and pepper to taste.

Before serving you can get all fancy and garnish the bisque with chiffonaded kale to give a nice pop of color.

Vegan Cornbread

Ingredients

2 cups cornmeal
1 cup unbleached all-purpose flour
2 teaspoons baking powder
1/3 cup coconut oil (melted/liquid)
2 tablespoons maple syrup
2 cups almond milk (room temperature)
2 teaspoons apple cider vinegar (or fresh squeezed lemon juice)
1/2 teaspoon salt

Directions

Combine the milk and apple cider vinegar (or lemon juice) in a medium-sized bowl and whisk together. Set aside.

Combine all dry ingredients together (cornmeal, flour, baking powder and salt) in a medium-sized bowl and stir until well combined.

Add the melted coconut oil and maple syrup to the milk mixture and whisk until foamy and bubbly.

Mix the wet ingredients with the dry ingredients and stir until well combined. (The batter will be somewhat thick).

Use a spoon or spatula to transfer the batter into an 8 x 8 glass baking dish.

Bake at 350 degrees for approximately 30 - 35 minutes.

Candied Lime Sweet Potatoes

Serves Four

Ingredients

2 Sweet Potatoes, peeled
1/2 Cup Sugar
1 tsp Molasses
1/2 tsp Salt
1 Tbs Fresh Lime Juice (no bottled stuff!)
Zest from 1 Small Lime
1/2 tsp Minced Ginger or 1/4 tsp Ginger Powder, optional
Black Pepper, to taste
Earth Balance, for dotting
Parsley or Cilantro, for garnish

Directions

Preheat oven to 400° F.

Thinly Sliced Sweet PotatoesSlice sweet potatoes thinly, about 1/8″,
with a mandoline or a food processor. Mix remaining ingredients
(except pepper, earth balance and garnish) together to form a paste.
Coat the sliced sweet potatoes well with the lime sugar mixture.

Arrange the coated slices in overlapping rows in one layer in an
oiled casserole dish. Dot with earth balance, sprinkle with pepper,
and wrap tightly with two layers of aluminum foil.

Bake for 30 minutes. Remove foil and bake uncovered for an
additional 10 minutes. It's okay if it looks a little watery when you

remove the foil, it'll reduce and form a nice glaze during the rest of the baking. Finish under the broiler to brown the top. Sprinkle with parsley/cilantro and serve immediately.

Caramelized Beets

Ingredients

2 lbs beets, peeled and sliced into 3/4 inch chunks
2 tablespoons olive oil
1/4 teaspoon salt
2 tablespoons balsamic vinegar (plus extra for drizzling)

Directions

Preheat oven to 375 F. Line a large rimmed baking sheet with parchment paper.

On the baking sheet, too the beets with olive and salt, to coat. Place in the oven and bake for 50 minutes, tossing every 20 minutes. Drizzle on the balsamic, toss the beets to coat, and cook for 10 more minutes.

Serve warm and drizzle with extra balsamic to taste.

Green Beans With Lemon-Almond Pesto

Ingredients

cooking spray
1 1/2 lbs. green beans, trimmed
1/2 c. almonds
1 garlic clove
1 tbsp. lemon juice
1 tbsp. extra-virgin olive oil
salt and pepper to taste

Directions

Preheat oven to 400 degrees.

Spray a rimmed baking sheet with cooking spray. Place beans on sheet in a single layer and spray tops with additional cooking spray. Roast for 15 minutes or until tender.

Combine almonds, garlic, lemon juice, olive oil, salt, and pepper in food processor and process until roughly chopped. Spoon over green beans before serving.

Red Quinoa Pilaf with Kale and Corn

Ingredients

1 cup red quinoa, rinsed in a fine sieve
3 cups prepared vegetable broth or 3 cups water with 1 vegetable bouillon cube
1 bunch kale (about 8 ounces)
2 tablespoons extra-virgin olive oil
4 to 6 cloves garlic, minced
3 to 4 scallions, white and green parts, thinly sliced
2 cups cooked fresh corn kernels
2 jarred roasted red peppers, cut into strips
2 tablespoons lemon juice, or more, to taste
1 teaspoon sweet paprika
1 teaspoon ground cumin

½ teaspoon dried rosemary

Salt and freshly ground pepper to taste

Directions

Combine the quinoa with 3 cups broth in a medium saucepan. Bring to a rapid simmer, then cover and simmer gently until the broth is absorbed, about 15 to 20 minutes. If the quinoa isn't quite done, add an additional ½ cup broth (or water) and continue to cook until absorbed.

Strip the kale leaves away from the stems. Discard the stems, or slice them very thinly. Cut the kale leaves into narrow strips. Rinse well and set aside.

Meanwhile, heat the oil in a large skillet or stir-fry pan. Add the garlic and sauté over low heat until golden.

Add the kale, stir together, and cover; raise the heat to medium and cook until wilted, about 2 to 3 minutes.

Add the remaining ingredients and cook, stirring frequently for 4 to 5 minutes longer. Transfer to a serving container and serve at once, or cover until needed.

Glazed Lentil Walnut Apple Loaf, Revisited

Ingredients

1 cup uncooked green lentils
1 cup walnuts, finely chopped and toasted
3 tbsp ground flax + 1/2 cup water
3 garlic cloves, minced
1.5 cups diced sweet onion
1 cup diced celery
1 cup grated carrot
1/3 cup peeled and grated sweet apple (use a firm variety)
1/3 cup raisins
1/2 cup oat flour
3/4 cup breadcrumbs
2 tsp fresh thyme (or 3/4 tsp dried thyme)
salt & pepper, to taste (I use about 3/4 tsp sea salt + more Herbamare)
red pepper flakes, to taste

Balsamic Apple Glaze:

1/4 cup ketchup
1 tbsp pure maple syrup
2 tbsp apple butter (or unsweetened applesauce in a pinch)
2 tbsp balsamic vinegar

Directions

1. Preheat oven to 325F. Rinse and strain lentils. Place lentils into pot along with 3 cups of water (or veg broth). Bring to a boil and

season with salt. Reduce heat to medium/low and simmer, uncovered, for at least 40-45 minutes. Stir frequently & add touch of water if needed. The goal is to over-cook the lentils slightly (see pictures in post). Mash lentils slightly with a spoon when ready.

2. Toast walnuts at 325F for about 8-10 minutes. Set aside. Increase oven temp to 350F.

3. Whisk ground flax with water in a small bowl and set aside.

4. Heat a teaspoon of olive oil in a skillet over medium heat. Sautee the garlic and onion for about 5 minutes. Season with salt. Now add in the diced celery, shredded carrot and apple, and raisins. Sautee for about 5 minutes more. Remove from heat.

5. In a large mixing bowl, mix all ingredients together. Adjust seasonings to taste.

6. Grease a loaf pan and line with parchment paper. Press mixture firmly into pan. Whisk glaze ingredients and then spread half on top of loaf. Reserve the rest for a dipping sauce.

7. Bake at 350F for 40-50 minutes, uncovered. Edges will be lightly brown. Cool in pan for at least 10 minutes before transferring to a cooling rack. I usually wait until loaf is cool before slicing.

Baked Leek and Sweet Potato Gratin

Ingredients

3 medium leeks, white and light green parts chopped (6 cups)
1 ½ Tbs. olive oil, divided
3 cloves garlic, minced (1 Tbs.)
3 Tbs. chopped fresh rosemary, divided
2 medium sweet potatoes (2 lb.), peeled and cut into ⅛-inch-thick slices
⅓ cup low-sodium vegetable broth
3 Tbs. Italian seasoned dry breadcrumbs
2 Tbs. finely grated Romano cheese, optional

Directions

1. Preheat oven to 450°F. Coat 10-inch round pan with cooking spray.

2. Heat 1 Tbs. oil in nonstick skillet over medium-high heat. Add leeks, garlic, and 1 1/2 Tbs. rosemary; sauté 8 minutes, or until softened. Season with salt and pepper, if desired.

3. Arrange one-third sweet potato slices over bottom of prepared pan, overlapping slightly. Spread half of leek mixture on top. Arrange another one-third sweet potato slices over leeks; top with remaining leeks, followed by remaining sweet potatoes. Drizzle broth over dish. Cover pan with foil, and bake 35 minutes.

4. Stir together breadcrumbs, remaining 1 1/2 tsp. oil, remaining 1 1/2 Tbs. rosemary, and Romano cheese, if desired, in small bowl. Remove foil from gratin, and sprinkle with breadcrumb mixture. Bake, uncovered, 15 minutes, or until breadcrumbs are browned and crisp. Let gratin cool slightly before cutting into 8 wedges and serving.

Vegan Pumpkin Pie Ice Cream

Ingredients

1 cup roughly chopped pecans or walnuts

2 tbsp brown sugar

1-15oz can pumpkin

1 pint container of French Vanilla Coconut Milk Creamer (we use So Delicious)

1 cup vanilla flavored unsweetened non-dairy milk (here we used So Delicious Cashew Milk)

1-6oz container of vanilla coconut milk yogurt (we use So Delicious)

⅓ cup sunflower oil

2 tbsp maple syrup or agave nectar

1½ tbsp pumpkin pie spice (or to taste. This amount will give the ice cream a pretty strong spice flavor!)

½ tsp guar gum (optional) (See note)

1 tbsp whiskey or bourbon if you prefer (optional) (See note)

Crushed cinnamon graham crackers for garnish

Directions

Combine pecans or walnuts and brown sugar in a small bowl. Mix well using your hands so the walnuts are coated. Cook at medium low heat in a non stick skillet for 3-5 minutes, stirring constantly. Set aside to cool

Combine all ingredients, except whiskey, in a blender and mix until well combined. Chill in the refrigerator for about 2 hours or overnight.

Once the ice cream base is chilled, add whiskey and mix well. Pour into an ice cream maker and churn until an ice cream like consistency is reached (time will vary depending the ice cream maker). Transfer to a bowl and mix in caramelized pecans.

Top with crushed cinnamon graham crackers before serving

Tip: Guar gum and whiskey give the vegan ice cream a softer and creamier consistency. You can omit these two ingredients, but keep in mind it will be slightly harder

Crustless Pumpkin Pie

Ingredients

1 tsp pumpkin pie spice
2 tsp cinnamon
1/2 tsp salt
2 tsp baking powder
1/3 cup flour (Almost any will work, including all-purpose gluten-free, but not coconut flour) (42g)
1/3 cup brown sugar (You can use a liquid sweetener. It'll just be a bit gummy) (53g)
pinch uncut stevia OR 2 extra tbsp brown sugar
1 (15-oz) can pumpkin puree
3/4 cup plus 2 tbsp milk of choice (210g)
2 tbsp oil, or omit and increase milk to 1 cup
1 tsp ener-g powder or 1 tablespoon ground flax (a commenter said cornstarch works, but I haven't personally tried it.)
2 1/2 tsp pure vanilla extract

Directions

Preheat oven to 400 F, and grease a 10-inch round pan. In a large mixing bowl, combine first 7 ingredients, and stir very well. In a separate bowl, combine all liquid ingredients with the energ or flax, and whisk. Pour wet into dry, stir to combine, then pour into the pan and bake 35 minutes. (It'll still be gooey after baking, but that's ok.) Allow to cool completely before transferring uncovered to the fridge to "set" for at least 6 hours before trying to slice.

Maple Pecan Pie

Ingredients

1/2 cup sugar
1/2 cup brown sugar
1/2 cup pure maple syrup
1/4 cup non-hydrogenated margarine
6 oz extra firm silken tofu (1/2 of a tetra pack)
1/4 cup cold unsweetened plain non-dairy milk
2 tablespoons cornstarch
1/2 teaspoon salt
1 teaspoon vanilla extract
2 cups pecan halves

Directions

Prepared Single Pastry Crust, pressed into a tart pan or pie plate (no need to parbake)

First we're going to make a caramel. In a 2 quart sauce pan, mix together sugars and maple syrup. Heat over medium heat, stirring often with a whisk. Once small bubbles start rapidly forming, stir pretty constantly for about 10 minutes. The mixture should become thick and syrupy. It shouldn't be boiling too fiercely, if it starts climbing the walls of the pan in big bubbles then lower the heat a bit.

Add the margarine, and stir to melt. Turn the heat off, transfer mixture to a mixing bowl. In the meantime, prepare the rest of the filling, working quickly so that the caramel doesn't completely set.

Crumble the tofu into a blender or food processor, along with the milk, cornstarch and salt. Puree until completely smooth, scraping down the sides of the blender to make sure you get everything.

Preheat oven to 350 F.

With the caramel still warm in the mixing bowl, add in the tofu mixture and the vanilla, and mix well. Fold in the pecans to incorporate.

Transfer to prepared pie crust and bake for 40 minutes. The pie is going to be somewhat jiggly, but it should appear to be set.

Let cool for a few hours, slice and serve! No cheating and pulling pecans off the pie.

Pumpkin Spice Rice Pudding

Ingredients

1 cup arborio rice, rinsed
1 1/2 cups almond milk
1 cinnamon stick
1/2 teaspoon salt
1 teaspoon orange zest
1/2 cup coconut sugar (regular granulated works fine too)
2 tablespoons coconut milk or almond milk
1 cup pumpkin puree
1/8 teaspoon ground cloves
1/8 teaspoon nutmeg
1/4 teaspoon allspice
Dash ground cinnamon
1/2 teaspoon fresh grated ginger
1/3 cup golden raisins (optional)

Directions

In a 2 quart saucepan, combine the rice, 1 1/2 cups almond milk, cinnamon stick, orange zest and sea salt. Over high heat, bring rice to a boil and then immediately reduce heat to low and cover. Cook 20 minutes, or until liquid has been absorbed. Keeping at low heat, stir in the rest of the ingredients and cook about 5 to 7 more minutes. Refrigerate until cold.

Serve with cashew cream or vegan whipped topping and a sprinkle of cinnamon. Makes 4 servings.

Printed in Great Britain
by Amazon